Partnering with your Hostess

Printed in U.S.A.
ISBN 0-9727491-1-X

Eighth Printing

Cover Design by Aimee Genter

Lifeline Press
2738 NE 9th Avenue
Portland, OR 97212

Partnering with your Hostess

Pathway to Recruiting Success

by
Steve Wiltshire

edited by Lynda Garner

LIFELINE PRESS

Acknowledgments

This work could not have been completed without the inspiration and assistance of the following people:

All my customers, hostesses, representatives, and leaders who taught me what I needed to know to write the content in this book;

All my seminar participants past, present, and future, who have and will bring my work to fruition;

Daphne Mathew, Sherry Trimble, and Vicky Boucher, my friends and business executives, who led our organization to the top;

Shirley, Arthur, and Scott LeVin, whose caring support over the last twelve years exceeded all my expectations;

Susan Moss, for mentoring me, especially during those long sessions on our all-expense-paid travel vacations;

The wonderful leaders of several companies in the Pacific Northwest, whose groups and businesses grew from the implementation of the principles and practices in this book;

And Julie Gentzler, who read my material in the early days and followed it step by step onto the stage as the #1 salesperson in the nation at her national convention.

To each of you I express heartfelt thanks.

CONTENTS

Part One: The Value of Partnering With Your Hostess

Part Two: Up Close and Personal Follow-Up

Part Three: The Application Of Person-to-Person Coaching

Appendices

Part One:

The Value of Partnering with your Hostess

"For the dream of yesterday
is the hope of today
and the reality of tomorrow."

—Anonymous

Blueprint for Success

Have you ever wanted a piece of someone's life, or for that matter, wanted something they had? Actually, don't you believe we see our own potential through observing the lives of others? We long to have fulfillment in our careers, a life-style congruent to our vision, and relationships that give meaning and purpose to our lives.

The *Dream* is one of the most alluring aspects of this industry. When we see others living it, we see possibilities of a similar, fulfilling experience for ourselves. I believe we each have within us the seed of greatness and the potential to achieve any goal we desire. Our stumbling blocks come from the circumstances that fog our vision of the path from *here* to *there*, and they start with thinking that there is *better* than here.

Dreams are important because they keep us moving into our greatness with endless vision of possibilities. Even more important, achieving a life well lived depends on choosing to see the good or the meaning in all experiences, thereby enjoying as much of the journey as possible.

Truly enjoying the journey *begins* with that decision but is attained only by action. But even decision and action aren't enough if we don't know how to get where we're going. A plan is needed. Vision and action are born from desire. The plan is developed by researching, asking questions, and striving to understand how and why things work.

Our first action must be to design the plan, a *blueprint*—a foolproof map or system that will produce results. This blueprint guarantees success, giving us peace of mind as we move into making our vision a reality.

A good blueprint is most often a version of a method of success that is tried and true. When we follow this proven plan, it guarantees results. It becomes the enduring guide to enjoying all aspects of our journey toward manifesting our dreams.

In these pages, I offer you what has truly been the foundation, not only of my own success, but also of those whom I have been so fortunate to lead. It is a complete way of working that will bring forth success in every area of your business. This book reveals this simple method, which created consistent achievement in my personal business as well as in our entire organization.

It is the method of **Person-to Person Coaching**. By committing to this wisdom, you will experience success. It will create a ripple effect as you share the business with others, enabling you to duplicate yourself over and over again while building an organization of consistent sales representatives.

As I wrote this material I was reminded of the hundreds of cancellations, rescheduled shows, and inconveniences that used to arise due to my lack of knowledge. Our industry is exciting but it is far from systematic.

Most of the time, 80% of our activities are getting 20% of our results.

We just continue doing things the same way because we simply don't know better, or we're just happy to be having fun while we're making money. It was my desire for success and my love of direct sales that gave me the endurance to persevere during that period of adversity.

I wrote this book for those of us who desire enjoyment in our careers, fulfillment in our business relationships, and procedural systems that result in astonishing numbers.

Most importantly, it is for those of us who desire to leave a legacy with our followers: the blueprint they need to live out their deepest desires and achieve their dreams.

"Life's challenges
are not supposed to paralyze you,
they're supposed to help you discover
who you are."

—Anonymous

My Introduction to Person-to-Person Coaching

By the time I reached my middle twenties, I had established my own way of conducting business and was fairly unwilling to accept advice from anyone. I was already a top producer nationally, selling $80,000–$90,000 annually and recruiting a minimum of 25 new representatives per year.

Although I had financial success, I lacked what I now know are the most important commodities in life: time and balance. My first marriage failed as a result of not applying time to the relationship.

If there is one truth I want to express in this book, it is the importance of living our deepest values.

When we don't honor our values, we rob ourselves of the aspects of life that create true happiness.

My wife Lynn and I were working very hard to be successful, when in 1990, my leader introduced me to the idea of meeting a hostess one-on-one to coach her for a successful show and pick up her guest list. At first, all I could envision was more work and more time. I didn't understand how this simple practice would someday profoundly change the course of my business. I resisted the concept and didn't have any interest in promoting it to my organization.

Even then, I knew there had been times in my career when I lost sight of my dreams and my belief in the industry. I can remember meeting guests at parties, making a connection with them, and visualizing successful future shows. The guests who booked during the evening were enthusiastic, and I left many of my parties on cloud nine, anticipating success.

Then the challenges would start: no return call from the hostess, no returned list, and the show would either cancel or reschedule. Consequently, my date book was often unbalanced and unmanageable.

It is said that insanity is doing the same thing over and over again and expecting to get different results. It was time for something new.

Lynn and I set out to design a program that fulfilled every need we identified in our lives and our business. As a result of the plan that we created, 95% of all our shows held on their original dates.

Our hostesses became more than clients, they became friends. Our show average increased, and recruiting became a consistently successful and natural part of our business. Not only was our personal business enhanced, our organization also grew from implementing this business practice.

As Lynn and I worked and taught our new program, Person-to-Person Coaching, we were often the beneficiaries of our hostesses, who would go above and beyond the call of duty in supporting our business. We believe it was due to our sincere interest in our hostesses, as well as the personal service we so willingly gave.

During the first months of the Person-to-Person Coaching program, we noticed a definite difference in the enthusiasm and participation of the hostess. Whether it was planning a special theme party for her friends, or her enthusiasm for earning her favorite items free, it was obvious that our hostesses were excited about their future party experience.

It was as if my entire belief in the business was reborn as a result of Person-to-Person Coaching.

The business and potential had always been there. It was the *blueprint* that had been missing. By completely committing to the principles of the program, I began consistently creating the success I wanted.

For years, I held five shows a week—either starter shows for new representatives or personal shows. My hostesses scheduled their shows within 30 days and always met with me to plan their parties and return their lists. Many times I received referrals from my hostesses as a result of their having heard my story and witnessed my passion for the industry.

Even more fulfilling were the rich relationships that came as a result of committing to Person-to-Person Coaching practices. It seemed as if the short thirty-minute appointment with the hostess prior to her show created a totally different kind of connection between us.

I particularly noticed how this new connection manifested at the show itself. I saw it in how the hostess included me in conversations, in how she introduced me to her friends, and in how she showed her support for me by encouraging others to schedule a party or join the business.

The bottom line is the system worked. It was evident in my personal shows, personal recruiting, group performance, and profits.

When my organization grasped the concept, my income exploded to well over six figures. I recall at least six conventions when Lynn and I took the #1 position in recruiting, the #1 position in personal sales for our level, and the #1 position for our level in group sales and group recruiting. This was the reward for following our blueprint.

What you are about to embark on is an in-depth look at the psychology of building relationships with our hostesses—person-to-person. Sometimes what seems like an unnecessary expenditure of time, is in fact, just what is needed to create a reality beyond one's limitations. A synergistic partnership far surpasses working alone.

PERSONAL SALES QUIZ

Score yourself! Read the following statements and evaluate your responses by using a point system. 1 represents not true at all and 5 represents absolutely true. 2 is closer to not true and 4 is closer to true. (3, of course, means you have absolutely no feeling at all about the matter and is probably not true.)

1. I'd feel so enthusiastic if my hostess would take the time to create a fun, entertaining atmosphere for her guests, providing festive surroundings to encourage their participation. ______

2. I would enjoy creating a mutually beneficial relationship with my hostess by meeting with her prior to her show to plan her party and share the benefits of joining my business, especially if it was for lunch, happy hour or dessert! ______

3. I'd be exhilarated if every hostess gave me an invitation list with 21 names and addresses, including postage, within one week of the time I scheduled her show.

______

4. I'd be most happy if I received from every hostess a referral of someone they felt would be talented in my business. _____

5. Yes, I'd be in the money if I recruited one out of every 8 hostesses I booked for a show. _____

6. I'd be downright ecstatic if 95% of all my bookings held on the date the hostess and I originally scheduled. _____

7. I would be "loving" my hourly wage if I were selling even 20% more than I am right now. _____

8. Sure, I'd give shows to my recruits on a split-profit program if I were booking 2 or 3 parties at every show. _____

9. I would feel honestly grateful if every hostess treated me like one of her friends at her party. _____

10. I'd have a ton of fun doing my show presentation if I had 10–12 guests at every party. _____

If your score averaged 4 or 5,
YOU'RE READY FOR THE SHIFT!

These "if" statements will become realities as soon as Person-to-Person Coaching is practiced on a regular basis. Imagine for a moment that you are already experiencing success in all these areas, and that you are actually living out the results described in each situation. How would you feel? How would your business change? Would your commitment level change?

Now, consider for a moment what it would be like for you to read this book in its entirety with an open mind. I invite each of you, experienced or beginner, to read these pages as if you were new to the business.

Put aside your past perceptions and open up to new possibilities. Are you ready for the blueprint—the "how to" leading you to accomplishing a higher show average, new recruits, more bookings. and most importantly, real enjoyment in your career?

Person-to-Person Show Set-Up: Get It All in Three Easy Steps

Imagine that during your presentation, a guest agrees to schedule a party. We invite you to begin by thanking each guest who agrees to schedule a show, whether they do so at the beginning or the end of your presentation. At the same time, ask them to reserve 10 minutes for you prior to leaving, so you can set them up for their party. You may say something like this:

> "Karen, you have so many items on your wish list. Let's schedule a show, get these items for free, and gather your friends together for a Friends' Night Out Party."
>
> *"Ok, Steve, sounds great, but I can't schedule my party until next month."*
>
> "Give me ten minutes before you need to leave, Karen, and I'll give you all the details. You and I will plan a fun experience for your friends."

Notice I did not have you deal with the booking right then. It's important for you to stay focused and at ease during your show presentation. The middle of your presentation and even the shopping period are not wise choices for setting up a new booking. It interrupts the flow of your current show, which in the long run, may decrease your bookings.

Acknowledge your new hostess and prepare yourself for the "person-to-person show set up" at the *conclusion* of the party. This will create the right environment for effective results.

Of course, there have been times when a guest who asked to book a show needed to leave during the middle of the shopping period, and I chose to give precedence to setting up the future show. This choice was based on the space in my date book, my priority in obtaining future bookings, and my assessment of how the current party was going.

Imagine a full list of names and addresses, including postage, returned to you within one week of scheduling each new show!

In order for this to happen consistently, you need to decide what you will offer your hostesses for completing this task. Some companies offer "thank you gifts" for returning an invitation list; some companies have extra credit benefits or incentive items that representatives can purchase for this use.

Creating the desire in the hostess to return her guest list is vital, because it is the guest list that actually *secures* the date and is the foundation for successful attendance.

If you are not sending invitations for your hostesses, I can almost guarantee that about 35% of your shows are either postponing or canceling.

If you *are* sending invitations but are not having your hostesses pay postage, your postage bill for 3 shows a week could be costing you over $1,000 a year. What would you do with an extra $1,000 a year? There are gifts you can offer for a couple of dollars that will reduce this amount drastically.

Regardless of which incentive you give your hostess, it is essential to follow this system for receiving a returned list.

Our focus here is for you to get clear about the gift you will offer a hostess for completing a guest list of at least 15 names and addresses, including postage, and providing it to you within one week of the time you set the date for the show.

Our second focus is that you make a decision to meet with every hostess within one week of the time you date their show to pick up their list and plan a fun party.

If you have not been introduced to this concept, you will clearly understand the psychology and power behind this business practice as you move deeper into the book. Right now is a great time to begin new business practices that will forever change the results and success of your business.

An intention behind every show is to secure future bookings. For every new booking you want two dates: a show date within thirty days, and a planning date within one week.

I always preferred setting these dates with my new hostesses individually, as opposed to setting them up in pairs or groups. This gave me time to create a stronger connection and handle any objections. As stated earlier, I generally scheduled my new hostesses at the conclusion of the shopping period.

Setting these two dates is crucial and it is during this phase that most representatives make their errors. They either offer to call the hostess the next day or week, or the new hostess takes control of the conversation and leaves without scheduling.

Both of these results are certainly not Plan A, are they? As you increase your knowledge, confidence, and ease with the language, so will you increase your results.

As a trainer and coach, I often ask representatives in our field, *"How many parties do you book at an average show?"*

Most respond by saying, *"two, sometimes three."*

My next question is, *"How many shows do you have up in the next 30 days?"* I am always amazed by their answers, which are usually nowhere near what my calculations would predict if they were actually booking those multiple shows with secured dates.

This tells us one of three things: they're not averaging the number of bookings they say they are, their follow-up is inadequate, or they *do* get the bookings at the show but the bookings don't hold. Many representatives make contact with guests who say they'll schedule a show, but who don't set a date. If that sounds like your experience, then we urge you to follow these simple guidelines.

Sometimes we are fatigued and a little unfocused at the end of an energetic party and the only thought going through our mind is, "I'm ready to go home, NOW!"

From this time forward, when that happens, I want you to tune into that part of yourself that remembers what you value about this work in the first place. Stop, get centered, get enthusiastic, and go set your dates for your upcoming shows.

Find yourself ready to move into a new energy of appreciation, self-confidence, and excitement by acknowledging your new hostess with a handshake or a hug. Look straight into her eyes and unabashedly offer your sincere appreciation as you thank her.

I encourage you to practice using language similar to the following:

"Jan, I want to express my appreciation to you for scheduling a show for me and (*tonight's hostess*). I'm so excited to have YOU as one of my upcoming hostesses. Our goal is a fun night out with friends.

I want to be clear about how you receive the hostess gifts and bonuses, and how (*tonight's hostess*) receives credit for your booking. All it's going to take is three basic steps."

"First, set your party date within 30 days of today. In a moment, I'll show you the dates I have available."

"Second, I'm sending you home with a blank guest list. I have a great invitation to send to all your guests, and I have a special gift for you when I receive your completed list of 15 names, addresses, and postage within one week." *(Share the gift or wrap it up and keep it a mystery)*. "Begin by calling all your guests to invite them to a fun, relaxed Friends' Night Out Party. Ask them for their addresses so we can mail them an invitation with a ticket for a special drawing. If you'd like to invite more than the required

15, great! In fact, you're welcome to hand deliver some of your invitations, but earning the special gift still requires submitting a completed list of 15 names, addresses, and postage."

"Third, we'll set up a time you and I can connect within this next week for a cup of coffee or a soda. At that time, I'll collect your list and together we'll plan a fun experience with your friends. I'll register your show with (company name) tomorrow. Then I have one week to pick up your list, and you'll receive the specials being offered to new hostesses."

I've often said, "It's all in the language." Years ago, I learned the value of giving the *future* hostess full ownership of the gift being awarded to the *current* hostess.

Tell her, *"I am so honored you've decided to host a show. You have an opportunity to give Yvonne (current hostess) a friendship gift by simply holding your show within the next 30 days.*

Guess what you'll earn for hosting your show within 30 days and returning your guest list to me within one week?"

Phrasing it this way will give her a sense of accountability and secure her commitment.

Now, just a word about time management. Prior to your shows, become fully aware of your own schedule for the upcoming seven to ten days. Ask your new hostess where she lives and works.

I have found it most convenient to meet with new hostesses immediately prior to other shows, generally between 5:00 and 5:30 p.m. Most of my shows were scheduled at 6:30 or 7:00, giving me time beforehand to meet with a future hostess.

Doesn't it make sense to coach your new hostesses on the same days you're conducting shows, especially if you already work 9:00 to 5:00? If you leave work at 4:30 or 5:00, you can treat yourself to a quick dinner, meet with your future hostess and then be on your way to your show.

If morning is better and it works for your future hostess, great!

Arrange the meetings near your home, work, or destination immediately thereafter.

It may take a little juggling on your part, but believe me, the rewards will exceed the effort. I am convinced that you will save time in the long run.

After you have set up the time to meet with your hostess and have explained the invitation list, have her choose a date for her show from your Party Date Cards. Use these cards to ensure that the hostess schedules a date that you, the representative, *want* to work. At the top of the three or four Party Date Cards simply write dates you would like to schedule. Have your hostesses choose one and fill out the pertinent information. I'm offering this method to you because I am utterly convinced it will bring you results.

✧ PARTY DATE ✧

Date: ____________ Day: ____________ Time: __________
Name: ____
Address: ____
City: __________________ State: ______ ZIP: __________
Home Phone: _____________________________________
Work Phone: _____________________________________
Best time to be reached: ________________________

Show Planning Date: _______________________________
Place: ____________________________ Time: __________

Hostess Booked From: ______________________________

Those are the steps: one, two, three. Set a show date for within thirty days; assign the task of completing the guest list; and schedule a date within one week to further connect one-to-one with the hostess, pick up the list, and plan the party.

This system of securing a booking is simple and professional, and it begins to create the sense of partnership with your hostesses. Throughout this book you will continue to learn the psychology of partnering with your hostesses and the benefit it provides you in life and business.

Part Two:

Up Close and Personal Follow-Up

“The meeting of two personalities
is like the contact
of two chemical substances;
if there is any reaction,
both are transformed.”

—Anonymous

It's All About Relationship

What happens after you set a date with your future hostess? What do you say if she *doesn't* set a date or wants you to call her to schedule later? What if a guest is *interested* in having a show, but wants to think about it for a couple of days. How would you effectively follow up with that hostess?

In *any* industry, communication is vital in creating lasting relationships with customers. In *our* industry, we create momentum with our shows that literally fuels a lifetime of business.

From one hostess to another, from a referral to a client, the business can be endlessly profitable. Lynn and I have traced show chains back to their original shows, which had held years earlier. It's an amazing phenomenon and it's all about momentum.

Momentum does not happen by accident; it is built by consistently and constantly applying tried and true business practices—following the blueprint. We build and develop business by communicating with our hostesses. The industry of direct sales refers to this communication as "follow-up."

Effective follow-up preserves future business and prevents cancellations. Have you ever had buyer's remorse? You purchased something you wanted or thought you wanted, and then days later you realized the product or service didn't have the value you originally thought it had.

Imagine how many hostesses have those same feelings. I'm sure many hostesses leave our parties saying to themselves, *"Why did I book a party?"*

Yes, it's *booking remorse,* and I'm here to assure you that there is a remedy. If you are committed to your blueprint, you may never have to deal with the booking remorse plague again.

"How can that be?" you may ask.

It's because your hostesses are going to commit to ***you*** *after they experience your professionalism and the personal way you follow up with them.*

By incorporating these teachings into your own style, you will exude confidence and authenticity, two irresistible traits.

I'd like to share with you a colorful, 3-D picture of how your principles can naturally create success. Years ago I was conducting an initial training class for a group of new representatives. I commonly started my classes with everyone sharing how they were introduced to the company.

Penny's story was an incredible affirmation of why I stand firm on the business practice of Up Close and Personal Follow-Up. She began by sharing that she had attended a party because it sounded like a great time. The hostess promoted a Mexican fiesta with margaritas and Mexican food. It was a Friends' Night Out, free of children, business and husbands.

Penny said, "*The party was fun and the director was enthusiastic and humorous. I decided to schedule my own party because I enjoyed the relaxed atmosphere and was impressed with how the representative interacted with the guests. But on my way home, as I contemplated why I had booked a show, I recalled my last two home parties. Both had only a few guests and were uncomfortable experiences. In fact, one of the representatives embarrassed me by the way she pressured my guests.*"

As Penny thought more and more about these two experiences, she decided to cancel her show. What changed her mind was the way the representative, Shirley, followed up on the show. Two days following the original party, she received a genuinely warm thank you card from Shirley that really impressed her. She said,

"I had planned on calling Shirley the next day to cancel my show, and then I received a beautiful thank you card. That in itself almost changed my mind, but it was actually the enthusiasm in her voice and her appreciative message when she called to confirm our meeting that convinced me to follow through with the party.

After we met to plan my party, I couldn't help comparing Shirley to the representatives who conducted my last two parties. She mailed invitations for my show; the last two representatives asked me to call my friends and didn't even offer invitations as an option. Shirley sent me a beautiful thank you card and actually took me out for coffee to plan my party. In fact, it was that person-to-person approach that got me thinking about joining the company."

Penny concluded by sharing again how impressed she was with how Shirley had followed up and how she communicated with her hostesses.

Now Penny's goal was to duplicate how Shirley conducted her business. Wouldn't *you* like a few recruits with similar stories and goals?

Experience Results With the Triple One System

As an executive trainer I discovered that most new representatives want a system that is easy to remember and easy to duplicate. I developed a system based on tried and true business follow-up practices. I call it the Triple One System and it will create consistency and simplicity in anyone's business.

In a nutshell, it begins with mailing a thank you card to the hostess ONE day after scheduling her show. Second, meet your hostess within ONE week after scheduling her show to pick up the completed guest list and plan the party. (This is the time for Person-to-Person Coaching.) Third, call your hostess ONE day prior to the party for directions to the party and last minute details. Implement the Triple One system in your business, starting with your very next show.

So let's backtrack for a moment. You're closing up the shopping period at your party and you have three bookings. Each new hostess has received a blank guest list from you with a request to complete it with guest names, addresses, and postage. You have also set up a date for each party, as well as times to meet each hostess to pick up her list and plan her show.

Now, what about the written details, the mundane work that creates success? Begin by writing the shows in your date book in pencil; hostesses' names, addresses, and home and work telephone numbers. Also write down the dates, times, and directions to your Person-to-Person Coaching appointments.

Consider starting a packet for each upcoming show. File them in date order with the current date in front. The show packet will eventually contain the Party Date Card, guest list, driving directions, hostess contact information, copies of customers' order forms, and a copy of the combined master order.

After the show is closed and submitted to the company, file these show packets in *alphabetical* order by hostess. This organizational habit will greatly affect your ease with the necessary paper work, and it will come in handy during special promotions or contests when you want to re-contact successful hostesses or particularly enthusiastic customers.

The Power of a Handwritten Thank You Card

The day after a show, mail all your new hostesses and any potential new hostesses a handwritten thank you card. It takes just a few minutes, and the habit is worth its weight in gold. Create a message utilizing the following guidelines:

1. Acknowledge your new hostess for giving the previous hostess credit.

2. Confirm the place and time of the Person-to-Person Coaching appointment.

3. Emphasize the importance of completing the guest list within one week.

4. Close the message by making a personal connection.

Here is an example:

Celeste,

Thank you for scheduling a party and supporting Mary in receiving her booking gift. Your enthusiasm at Mary's show was contagious. I'm looking forward to meeting you at Starbucks on Broadway, Tuesday, May 2nd at noon to pick up your list and plan your party. Don't forget, you receive a $30 bonus for bringing your completed guest list with addresses and postage to our appointment. This is your special night out with your friends. I'm so happy to be a part of it. Let's have a fun party together!

Live your dreams,

Steve

EXERCISE 1

How will you word your thank you card?

"The difference between
ordinary and extraordinary
is that little extra."

—Anonymous

THINK-ABOUT-IT PACKETS

Occasionally we meet a guest who is not yet ready to commit to having her own show. Often, I have been able to obtain an additional booking or two because I was willing to give the guest a little more time to ponder the possibility of a show.

I always handed out one to three Think-About-It packets, prior to the end of the show. Even if I had booked several shows, if there was an uncommitted guest I *wanted* to book, I handed her a Think-About-It packet.

I would say something like, *"Amy, I want you for a future hostess!"* or *"Girlfriend, we need to have a show! How do you feel about taking home a catalog and some information on hosting your own show? I'll call you in a couple of days. If you decide to schedule a party, I can still give Mary (the current show's hostess) credit for the booking. And if you decide not to, thank you for considering it."*

Most of the time the guest will gladly take the packet or give you the information you need for future use.

For example, Amy might say, *"Actually, Steve, I'd like to have a show; but I'm going to be on vacation for 6 weeks, and I can't schedule anything until September."*

If I hadn't asked, I would not have received this information, which was not a "no," but actually a "yes" for a later date.

Or Amy might respond, *"Now isn't exactly the best time for me. I'm really being challenged with some health issues, but I'll think about it. Call me on Saturday morning and I'll let you know."*

Here's an opportunity to make a personal and compassionate connection with someone who may be very much in need of friends and fun. A call to her on Saturday may result not only in a booking, but also in a mutually fulfilling experience of person-to-person contact.

I've always "chosen" my hostesses in advance, concentrating on guests I knew I would enjoy as hostesses.

Remember, your primary focus is to set a date, so offer something special to your hostesses for scheduling a party within 30 days and returning a completed guest list to you within one week.

On the next page is an example of a thank you card for a potential hostess who did not book at the party itself.

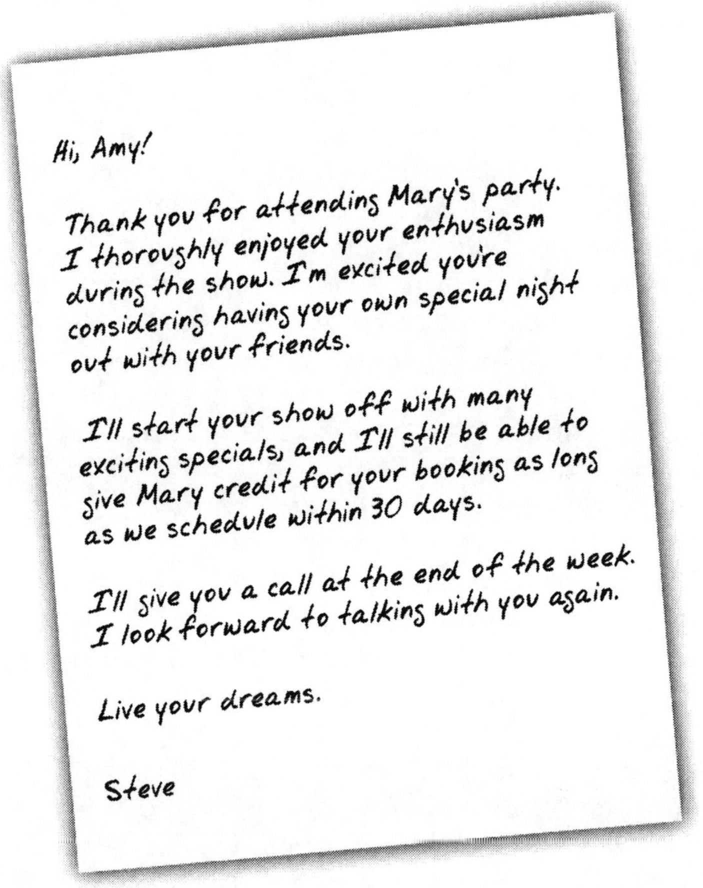

Hi, Amy!

Thank you for attending Mary's party. I thoroughly enjoyed your enthusiasm during the show. I'm excited you're considering having your own special night out with your friends.

I'll start your show off with many exciting specials, and I'll still be able to give Mary credit for your booking as long as we schedule within 30 days.

I'll give you a call at the end of the week. I look forward to talking with you again.

Live your dreams.

Steve

What do you do if your hostess just won't set a date? Well, frankly, it's time to stick to tried and true principles and guidelines. Although rules can be broken, that option should be a well-considered, conscious choice. Most of the time our principles should be honored; it's the agreements with ourselves that matter most.

If the hostess requests to set a date tomorrow or in a couple of days, you could compromise. For example, *"Karen, Mary (current hostess) earns credit for shows set within 30 days. I am closing the show this evening and will be submitting it to the company tomorrow. I would very much like to give you the extra credit for setting the date, as well as give Mary her credit for the booking. I'll tell you what, if you set a date for your show by Wednesday and meet me within one week, with your guest list fully completed, I'll honor the extra credit."*

Be sure to say it with fun and confidence in your voice. *Warning:* if this is happening to you often, take a look at your confidence level and your choice of language.

When setting a date, be professional and sincerely grateful. It is simply a necessary part of what the hostess must commit to do. Your naturalness and professionalism will make it easy for her. Communicate through direct eye contact, powerful language, and a huge smile.

Confirming the Person-to-Person Coaching Appointment

Part of any effective follow-up system is confirming appointments. Two days prior to each Person-to-Person Coaching appointment, extend a courtesy call to your hostess reminding her of your appointment and bonuses for bringing her completed invitation list. I preferred to talk to my hostess directly; but often I had to leave a message, which still completed my objective. These messages sounded something like this:

> "Hi, Susan, this is Steve. I'm looking forward to seeing you tomorrow at noon at Starbucks. I've had a busy week, and I'm ready for a fun, lighthearted time with you as we plan your party! I have lots of specials to share with you!
>
> Be sure to bring your completed invitation list and postage so I can give you extra credit. If you have any questions, reach me on my cell phone (leave number). See you tomorrow!"

I would say about one out of ten hostesses tried to reschedule with me. If they left a message, I called them back. I let them know that I had planned my morning or evening around their appointment and would be in that particular area, and I encouraged them to honor the appointment. I also reiterated the bonus for having their list to me within a week.

If I reached them in person, the conversation would sound something like this:

"Hi, Susan, this is Steve. I got your message: it sounds like you're having a challenging day."

"Hi, Steve. Yeah, I have a report that's due by 4:00 p.m. and I can't make our appointment at noon."

"I can really appreciate the stress level of deadlines. I scheduled my other appointments around our appointment today, so I'm in your area most of the day. Could I connect with you for a few minutes just to pick up your list and drop off your hostess packet? I registered your show last week, and our deadline is tomorrow to qualify you for the special bonus. Maybe we could meet in the lobby at your office for a few moments."

"OK, Steve, I'll meet with you for just a few minutes shortly after noon."

These are likely to be people who resist completing the guest list. Personally, I believe it is right to ask people, respectfully and non-judgmentally, to honor their commitments. If we become responsible in following through with our own commitments, doing what we say we will do, we will attract the same.

The guest list is paramount. Earlier I mentioned registering the list with the company. It is important to become savvy in your choice of words and phrases.

You need to understand that you ***are*** *the company.* ***You*** *are the representative of the company in your local area.*

Crafted phrases like *"I registered your show for (date)"* and *"I have until (date) to give you credit for your Invitation List"* will be very effective if you believe in their underlying truth. Remember, it's all about language, sticking to principles, and asking the hostess to honor her commitment. As for your part, the list is gold; offer something unique and desirable for it!

"Obstacles are those frightful things
you see when
you take your eyes off your goals."

—Anonymous

Obstacles?

What do you do if a hostess attempts to cancel her Person-to-Person Coaching appointment?

First, offer to cut the meeting short but still connect, as I just illustrated. Second, if physically meeting is not an option, I offer to meet my hostess the following day. However, if my own schedule is too tight for that, I request that she fax or e-mail the guest list prior to the end of the day, which will "still entitle her to receive *all* the bonuses." (If you don't own a fax machine, get one.) The last resort is to take the names and addresses over the phone.

Your top priority is to have the list in your possession within 1 day of the original time of the Person-to-Person Coaching appointment. Any longer than that greatly reduces your chance of ever obtaining a completed guest list.

What happens if you get to a Person-to-Person Coaching appointment and your hostess doesn't have her list completed?

First and foremost, remember she is there because she is interested and committed. She may not be organized, but she's committed. I believe most of us have good intentions. Life happens. Obviously she's busy or just not organized. Have compassion and connect with her. Keep it simple and stay within the parameters of your business principles.

Explain to her that she will still receive the bonuses and you will be the representative conducting the show, *as long as* you receive the list tomorrow. Ask her to fax the list to you. If that isn't possible, offer to take it over the phone.

How would you respond if you called to confirm the Person-to-Person Coaching appointment, and your hostess asked to reschedule because her list wasn't completed?

Sometimes this is the person who is a perfectionist, an over-achiever. Nothing is good enough unless it's completed or perfect; and if that is the case, they often switch to the direct opposite, not doing it at all. Be reassuring and keep it light.

Give her options. Tell her that she's got 24 hours to complete the list, perhaps like this, *"Jenny, grab the White Pages and get your addresses! If you don't have all of the addresses by tomorrow, it's ok. You can call a few of your guests and then fax or e-mail the additional addresses."*

What do you do if you get to the appointment and your hostess do show up?

This is a tough one, but it's a example of "life happens"; and we e have two choices. We either accept allow it to throw us off center.

First of all, did you confirm th appointment by phone the previous Would *you* keep an appointment tha confirmed? In today's society we all cell phone and voice mail in case of minute conflict. Your job is to check voice mail and/or your business rec before you leave for your appointmer

That said, when a hostess star up and we choose acceptance of the unexpected, it's like making a deposi integrity account. I believe that depo show up in another form, better and waiting for. It's an issue of trust and your truth.

Bring a book, write in your jou just relax. Honestly, don't we all com about not having enough time anywa Take advantage of this opportunity a create a moment for yourself!

Part Three:

The Application of Person-To-Person Coaching

"The road to success is dotted
with many tempting parking places."

—Anonymous

Making the Decision

As I think of the thousands of hostesses I have coached, it becomes clear that Person-to-Person Coaching is the one area that has had the largest impact on my success. But I must admit, it was the most difficult practice to commit to. Why was it so difficult?

Let's face it, when we feel overbooked, or experience a family conflict, or just don't feel like it, we all look for ways to avoid commitment. In the early years of implementing Person-to-Person Coaching, I'd schedule appointments to coach my hostesses in person; but then I'd change my mind and coach them over the phone because of last minute conflicts. When a hostess would try to cancel her appointment, or I had a conflict, I sometimes settled for a faxed list and a quick conversation.

Eventually, I learned how to successfully manage my schedule and fully commit to this practice. Lynn and I analyzed many successful shows and new recruits, and came to realize that Person-to-Person Coaching was greatly enhancing our recruiting success.

In our business Person-to-Person Coaching became almost synonymous with recruiting.

One fall, Lynn and I personally recruited 52 representatives. In fact, we recruited consistently every month for seven straight years. You will undoubtedly receive incredible results by implementing this method. But more importantly, you will have a great time doing it!

If you were to ask me what area of the industry I enjoy most, I would tell you my favorite role is training large groups of representatives, and that my second favorite activity is meeting hostesses for Person-to-Person Coaching. I am actually awestruck by how much I have learned about life conversing with hostesses. There is no doubt that these experiences have greatly improved my listening, communication, and presentation skills.

Now it's time for *you* to learn how to effectively coach your hostesses "person-to-person" for maximum results.

Are You Prepared?

What's in your hostess packet?

Hostesses very rarely look back through their hostess packets before their show, except to look at the catalog or use an order form for an outside order. Keep it simple. (Catalog, date card for an outside booking, hostess plan, any company or local special promotions, outside order forms, theme party flyer and your business card.)

Are you going to bring samples of your product?

Most hostesses wouldn't entertain the idea of having a party if they weren't interested in the product. Consider bringing a few samples of new products or hostess items.

I often met my hostesses in restaurants or coffee shops, knowing that someone would comment on my product. I always carried a few door prize slips. After receiving a compliment on my product from the waitress or a guest of the restaurant, I would extend them an invitation to enter my monthly door prize drawing.

Inevitably they would ask for a catalog. Purposely, I carried only enough catalogs for the hostess, which would allow the following scenario to take place:

> "Are you feeling lucky? Would you like to enter my monthly drawing?"
>
> *"Sure, thank you."*
>
> "Hi, I'm Steve and you are _____?"
>
> *"Oh, hi, I'm Cheryl."*
>
> "Cheryl, I'd offer you a catalog today, but I only brought enough for Karen. I'll give you a call and set up a time to drop by a catalog next week."
>
> *"Thanks, Steve. That would be great."*

Let's look at this situation. My focus was connecting with my hostess, Karen, at a Person-to-Person Coaching appointment. Then an opportunity arose to schedule a personal showing with Cheryl.

The *opportunity* was perfect; the *timing* was not. When opportunity knocks, open the door; but pursue it at the proper time. In this case, good timing meant inviting Cheryl to enter my drawing in order to obtain her name and number and call her later.

Many times your hostess will be the one to plant the seed by saying something totally authentic like, *"I'm so excited! I'm having my own party to earn that for free!"*

Are you bringing recruiting material to your Person-to-Person Coaching appointment?

If your intention is to create interest, be prepared to share your story briefly and hand out your favorite recruiting pamphlet. In just a few pages, you will learn how to design a way of sharing your recruiting story comfortably and authentically.

Have you considered creating a "Share Book"?

A Share Book gives a brief visual impression of all the features and benefits surrounding joining your company, such as literature on your profit program, kit specials, contests, management programs and personal successes. Share Books, made more personal with copies of check stubs from you or other representatives, will magnetize the interest of others.

Display pictures of travel trips and contest prizes offered by your company, especially ones you have earned. Share Books allow you to share your story with animation while engaging your audience (in this case, your hostess) in your company's benefits.

Are you prepared to arrive a few minutes early for your appointments?

Being early is vital. Take heed of this principle, especially if being consistently on time seems difficult for you. I've encountered situations where hostesses actually came to the appointment, and then left the scene because I was late. There are always reasons; but excuses won't give you creditability, recruits, or higher paychecks. It boils down to one very important value: *be on time!*

What Is Your Role As a Person-to-Person Coach?

Let me begin by telling you that while I have been writing this, I have had the recurring thought, *"Are you making the book too complicated? Is this too much information? Come on, Steve, coaching a hostess can be quite an easy task, can't it?"*

Here is what I know. For years I found myself thinking, *"Why can't they get it? It's not that difficult."* Well, actually, our industry is quite foreign to most; and it usually doesn't offer extensive training courses, or even consistent one-on-one training. Representatives learn the business here and there, bit by bit. My commitment is to give you all of it—everything I have—every little detail in its entirety.

I'm offering you the opportunity to pick and choose skills as you grow and expand in business and in life. I want to help you understand all aspects of my teachings, the complete version of the "who, what, where, when, and how."

Reaping the rewards of this career, the money, the experience, the fulfillment, has been easy for me only because I learned how. For me, it was a simple case of trial and error coupled with the will to move through adversity, and the desire to understand the business, that resulted in success.

You, too, will have to learn partly through trial and error; but it is my intent to equip you with tools that will enhance your possibility of success.

Now then, let's talk about your role, with the understanding that if you get to your appointment and you are only comfortable talking a little, sharing a little, picking up a guest list, and leaving, that's ok. You can always pursue the mastery version in months to come.

Think of the phrase "Person-to-Person Coaching." What does it mean to you? Essentially, it means you are a party coach; your role is to coach your client to have a successful party!

Today we find coaches in athletics, the performing arts, and in the fields of fitness and business. During the late 1980's a new kind of coach emerged, a "life coach." The role of the life coach is to provide the client with tools that enhance the clarity and performance in her or his whole life, often including business.

While Person-to-Person Coaching does not require the extensive training and certification common to life coaching, it is based on the same concept: create your own success.

You help the hostess design the ideal party, rather than just showing up and seeing what happens. As a party coach, part of your role is to be honestly curious about what the hostess really wants.

> *"Mary, what items do you want to earn with your free shopping from your show? Who would you really like to attend your party? What do you want this experience to provide for you?"*

Another part of your role is giving information to her, whether it's the hostess plan, or information on joining the company.

Much of your role is to dance in the moment with your hostess by being completely present to her. You will be asking questions, listening to the answers, and sharing the information that creates results for you and your hostess.

As important as understanding your role as coach is your intention for the coaching appointment.

You will achieve a result, whether it's the one you intended or not. How much more effective it is to clarify your intention for the experience beforehand.

Although connecting with the hostess, picking up the list, and setting a goal for a $500 show were always high on my list of priorities, my greatest intention during these sessions was to share the business with my hostess. With that in mind, I gathered as much information about my hostess as I could, so I could genuinely offer her the opportunities to obtain things she *really* wanted in life by joining the business.

After conversing with her for about ten minutes, I'd have a good idea of what was happening in her life, and I'd plant recruiting seeds she could identify with.

Part of my intention was to create an alliance with her, knowing she would promote her show if she felt good about *me,* as well as the entire party package, and that a successful show would greatly increase the possibility of her joining the company.

Your intention may not include recruiting right away, but as you become more experienced, you will recognize Person-to-Person Coaching as the most effective way to increase your organization.

What is your *intention* for your Person-to-Person Coaching appointments?

Building Your Coaching Muscles: Learning, Asking, and Suggesting

Where are we? Oh, that's right, we're five minutes early for our Person-to-Person Coaching appointment. We're dressed for success and we're ready to be present and enjoy our experience with our hostess.

What does "being present" mean to you? I'm sure it means something a little different to each of us. I define it as being in the moment, not in the past, and not in the future. The bottom line is to be on time, leave your problems in the car, and focus on where you are right now.

Get clear about your intention, yet be flexible. Your intention is to connect with your hostess, collect the invitation list, coach her for her show, and share your business opportunity.

Let's take a closer look at the actual agenda of Person-to-Person Coaching by breaking it down into timed segments. As we cover each segment, ask yourself these questions: *"If I were to cover this package with my hostess within 45 minutes to an hour, would my business change? Would it become more successful?"*

Commit to yourself, *"If, in fact, I do believe that applying this principle will bring about success, then I'm going to coach vigorously, with passion and faith."*

The first ten minutes are the most important. I can remember the days when I did a lot of talking and very little listening. How can we connect with our hostesses if we don't listen to them? I learned that if I took the time to listen to another person, a relationship would blossom.

It starts with knowing what questions to ask and then simply listening with sincere interest. The focus is to actually get to know your hostesses during the first ten to fifteen minutes.

During my many interaction seminars I have invited participants to partner with another participant in role-playing different segments of a Person-to-Person Coaching appointment. I found that most of them had talent in presenting information, such as explaining the specials, sharing the hostess plan, or creating a fun theme. But as I observed these sessions, it became obvious how many representatives in this industry lack confidence in casual conversation.

It is in the first ten minutes that a true connection can be made with your hostess. This is accomplished by simple, casual conversation.

During this time, I discovered a wealth of information about my hostess by simply asking a question and then listening to her response. Consider that making a connection with her is also of benefit to you in more ways than just business.

I started this technique about ten years ago because one of my mentors credited her amazing success in recruiting to the rapport she developed with each hostess during the first ten to fifteen minutes of the coaching. Naturally, when I first started implementing casual conversation during my hostess coaching appointments, it seemed like such a waste of time, but to my surprise, I found myself sincerely enjoying it.

Actually, I'm awestruck by all the shared stories that have enriched and empowered my life over the years. Now I understand why my mentor was a top, consistent recruiter. She gave a part of herself by listening and caring about others.

There's an old saying, *"People don't care how much you know until they know how much you care."* Interestingly enough, I started noticing how my hostesses began to listen to *me* after I spent time listening to *them.*

I am now convinced that if representatives in our industry spent more time conversing with and listening to their hostesses, all they would need to do to have successful shows is cover the simple basics.

Why? Because when your hostess cares about you, she'll promote you beyond your wildest expectations. Lynn and I consistently recruited several hostesses every month, because we knew who they were, what they wanted, and what was important to each of them.

Part of our essential human nature is to give. We're just wired up that way. When we give, we amplify our aliveness to life and become aware of our interconnectedness with others.

During these first ten to fifteen minutes, acknowledge your hostess by thanking her for hosting a show; and then follow up with a few basic questions.

- How do you like your job?
- Where do you work?
- Do you work during the day?
- What do you think of my job? *(This question could lead to interest in the business.)*
- Are you married? Children?
- Why did you decide to schedule a party?
- What do you want to earn free?
- What kind of experience would you like your party to be?

The idea is not to "grill" your hostess, but to open up a free exchange and make a connection.

It has been said that being listened to
is so close to being loved,
most people cannot tell the difference.

Do You Know How to Listen?

Listening is one very important way we can give of ourselves, and it is a skill that can be developed with practice. As human beings, we can actually listen at three different levels; and if we're aware of these levels, we can use them to increase the effectiveness of our communication.

The first level is *Personally-Focused Listening.* That is what we are doing when our attention is fully on ourselves and our own agendas, concerns, and considerations. We may hear the words of another person, but we're primarily involved in our own perceptions, judgments, feelings, needs, etc.

We may appear to be listening, but only a part of us is there. Sometimes our ability to listen is contaminated with past perceptions that influence what we think the outcome should look like.

Other times, we're so critical of ourselves that most of our energy is concentrated on our responses. *"Will this sound stupid? Will this sound right? Should I say it or not?"* When we are engaged in coaching hostesses, our concentration needs to be on *them—their* responses, *their* reactions, *their* needs.

Personally-Focused Listening is not bad. It is extremely important: for instance, when our bodies are trying to tell us it's time to eat, or our deeper selves are trying to remind us of our commitments.

This level of listening is very powerful when it is directed with intention. For example, you may set an intention to get up every morning and spend some time asking yourself, *"What will I accomplish today? How will my behavior be today? What can I do in each of my roles that will give me the greatest results?"* It is in listening to Self in this way that this level of listening fulfills its highest purpose.

When we are listening at the second level, *Relationally-Focused Listening*, our attention is focused outside ourselves entirely in one direction. Imagine listening to a small child. Because he may not speak very clearly, or because you may love her very much, your focus is fully directed toward that child, listening intently to every word.

When we choose to participate at this level of listening, we are completely tuned in, focusing on the message in the moment. One of the most important characteristics of top recruiters, and actually, top achievers in any field, is their ability to listen at this level. It is through *Relationally-Focused Listening* that we gather the necessary data to communicate at a higher level.

Universal Listening employs a soft focus that takes in everything around us. At this level we are aware of the energy exchange between ourselves and others, and how that energy is changing.

At this level, you are conscious of the underlying mood and impact of a conversation—where it is taking you and the other person. Stand-up comics have a highly developed sense of listening at this level, sensing the connection with the audience and the most effective timing for punch lines and stories.

The masters in our industry experience this level of universal listening while conducting their presentations.

They can sense how the show is being received and how the energy is building or dissipating. This gives them the opportunity to be flexible, appropriately shifting gears throughout their show.

For example, they may hear a comment made by a guest who needs to leave early, or notice the attention span of the group waning, and make changes in the moment to improve the end result. This is also the level at which intuition will be most available to you, including metaphor and imagery.

Personally-Focused Listening, Relationally-Focused Listening and *Universal Listening* are all important. Consider writing these three levels of listening on an index card you can carry with you. As we lead into the mechanics of hostess coaching, I invite you to increase your awareness of which level of listening you are using at any given moment.

If you have spent some time before your appointment engaged in *Personally-Focused Listening,* you will be ready to participate with your hostess at the *Relationally-Focused* and *Universal* levels.

Person-to-Person Affirmation Quiz

*At a recent seminar, I asked a participant to join me on stage to role-play the first fifteen minutes of a hostess coaching experience. Before we started our unrehearsed dialogue, I invited her to take a quiz simply by responding, "Yes, that is correct," to each statement. My primary focus was to empower her to incorporate each characteristic. As you read the following statements, empower yourself by saying out loud, **"Yes, I am"** or **"Yes, I do"** to each affirmation.*

1. You are an avid listener.
2. You are a genuine, caring human being.
3. You have a positive disposition.
4. You ask empowering questions.
5. You're curious about others. You want to know who they are.
6. You're always five minutes early.
7. You wear professional attire.
8. You have an intention, but you are also flexible.
9. You use your hostess's first name throughout the conversation.

Is it possible that these characteristics will draw others to you? Yes, I know so. As you build an alliance with your new friend, your hostess, you will notice a strong commitment and interest that could have been developed only from Person-to-Person Coaching.

The Step-by-Step Experience of Person-to-Person Coaching

1. Arrive five minutes early.

Give yourself five minutes to enter the *Relationally-Focused Listening* level and organize your literature. Bring the following necessities to your coaching appointment: date book, catalogs, company specials, Party Date Cards, company hostess plan, Order Forms (including outside order forms), recruiting information, theme party flyers and share book.

2. Acknowledge your hostess upon arrival.

First impressions are lasting! As your hostess arrives, greet her with authentic enthusiasm! Sometimes we are genuinely excited about meeting our new hostesses, but our nervousness or lack of ease gets in the way.

Acknowledging others should be practiced so it can be done with confidence and naturalness. Then your genuine enthusiasm and sincere interest in the hostess will be able to be seen and felt by those receiving it.

3. Casual conversation (about 10 minutes).

Earlier we discussed the importance of building an alliance with our hostesses during the first ten minutes of the coaching appointment. Several years ago, I began to express my appreciation for the hostess by thanking her for assisting me in achieving my current goal, usually a travel trip. This created career interest at the beginning of my coaching appointments.

Then, starting with her name, I asked her a simple, casual question, *"Lisa, how's your life going?"*

I borrowed this from my own life coach, because it truly resonated with me. I can't remember a time in my life when I felt more important than she made me feel during the beginning of our appointments. Perhaps it was her enthusiasm, or the newness of the experience itself; but whatever it was, I felt important.

It's simple and effective; acknowledge your hostess with sincerity and enthusiasm and ask something like, *"How's life?" or "How's it going?"*

Listen to the answer. It will engender a conversation that will give you much information about your hostess. It is through this information that you can lead her into the possibility of starting her own business.

4. Create a theme party and give your hostess an example of how to invite her guests (5 minutes).

This is where you move from *eliciting* information to *giving* information. *"Mary, let's plan a fun theme party for your guests. How about a Mexican Fiesta or a Happy Hour Party. Or do you feel more like a Wine-tasting Soiree or maybe a Saturday Continental Breakfast?"*

When a hostess schedules a theme party, it gives her another reason in addition to the product to invite her guests to a party. Even companies whose products are well known, household names draw more guests when a hostess promotes a theme.

After confirming a theme, begin to teach her how to invite her guests. It may sound something like this:

Karen, my goal is that your friends leave your party saying it was the most exciting home party they've ever attended. Whether we have 3 guests or 20, I'm committed to creating a fun experience with you and your friends. Here's how I would like you to invite your guests.

"Jenny, I'd like to invite you to a Friends' Morning Out party on August 17th at my place. My theme is a Saturday Continental Breakfast, and I'm going to have strawberry waffles, special coffees, champagne, and orange juice.

My friend, (*your name*), is a representative for (*company name*). She's going to bring her (*product*), and we're going to enjoy a morning of laughs and have a great time. She's a lot of fun and really makes the experience enjoyable.

By the way, feel free to bring a friend—maybe someone you haven't spent time with for a while. This will give you an opportunity to see your friend and hang out at my party."

I want you to understand the psychology in this message. Most hostesses desire a light, relaxed show that doesn't involve pressuring their friends or overselling a product. If you are *primarily* promoting a good time and *lightly* promoting the product, it gives the hostess the reassurance she can do the same.

I cannot count the number of times I've scheduled shows with guests who had never before hosted a home party.

During our conversations, I sensed they were not comfortable with the party plan "scene." My response was to emphasize the fun, relational aspects of the party.

One of my hopes is for you, too, to be able to book many guests who have never hosted a home show. When setting a date with a new hostess at a party, give her a similar example of how to invite her guests.

Many new hostesses don't follow through with their bookings simply because they are at a loss as to how to invite people to their party. Reinforce your helpful example at the Person-to-Person Coaching appointment. If you are coaching your hostesses within a week, chances are they will have invited only a few of their guests by then and will gain confidence from further gentle training.

5. Let's talk about your free goodies and specials (5 minutes).

All hostesses enjoy discussing their *free shopping*! Consider bringing a few samples of your products along with a Wish List form. It might look something like the example on the next page.

My name is: ______________________________

My address is: ______________________________

Home phone: ______________ Work Phone: ______________

My occupation: ______________ ☐ Full-Time ☐ Part-Time

Be a TALENT SCOUT!

Who do you know who needs MONEY and FUN?

NAME	PHONE

I AM INTERESTED IN **FREE**

☐ Product ☐ Information ☐ Events

MY WISH LIST:

ITEM AND PAGE #	SALE PRICE	BONUS ITEMS

Total Selections ______________

Shipping/Ins. ______________

Bonus Items ______________

Miscellaneous ______________

Total ______________

As you share your company's Hostess Plan, write down your hostess's favorite items on the Wish List. Hostess Plans vary in our industry; some offer very little, and some over-offer. It is vital that you fully understand your specific Hostess Plan in its entirety, as well as every special available to your hostess. *Your* role is to promote your Hostess Plan and your *hostess's* role is to choose her favorite items.

The Wish List is an incredible tool because it identifies all the items your hostess is interested in, which could provide a hefty customer order at show time. Also, if you refer to one or two of these items while talking with your hostess at her party, it will reinforce that you are sincerely interested in her.

Your focus is to create a successful show. Consider offering a special gift to hostesses who meet or exceed a specific goal. For instance, consider creating a $500 club or a $1,000 club. Offer a special gift to each hostess who meets this expectation. Another option is to invite them to a special celebration with bingo, drawings, or game prizes.

What should you offer? Consult your leader. Perhaps there is an incentive item for this purpose available through your company. Don't spend any more than $10 per item on this program; *it is truly unnecessary*. The intention is to find a popular item that motivates the majority of your hostesses to set and "go for" a specific goal.

What are you going to offer your hostess for bookings? Many companies offer hostess credits or gifts for three parties booked from a show, which encourages those bookings to actually hold.

But what if there is only one booking? If your company doesn't offer a gift or special purchasing opportunity for each individual booking, develop your own program without incurring additional expenses. The purpose is to provide the same incentive for fewer than three bookings and to encourage the hostess to reach for even more than three.

6. Outside orders (5 minutes).

If a hostess is motivated, one half of your show sales could be the result of outside orders! How would you feel if every show you held had as many outside orders as orders taken at the show itself?

It's true that some products are easier to sell in person and some products sell equally well from the catalog. As I analyze my twenty years of experience with two companies, it is clear that I had better success getting outside orders with one company than the other. However, if I step back and compare their overall programs, it is clear that each company has areas of strength that make it unique. *It is your job as a representative to promote your company's strengths.*

One of my coaching clients, who represents a line of clothing, wanted to be coached on how to increase her outside orders. As we looked at her company's programs, it became obvious that she would have little or no control over the outside order program.

Through strategizing, we were able to design a program that increased her contacts outside the show by simply offering the hostess additional credit for each outside, scheduled personal appointment. My client increased her bookings, personal showings, and show sales by concentrating on the *strengths* of her company's programs and *creating her own* individual plan to achieve outside orders.

Whether you have a catalog or not, or sell a collectable, decorative product or a must-see-in-person product, always ask your hostess for outside orders or names of her friends who would like to see the products in person.

As a rule, only 30-50% of the guests will actually attend the party. I'd like to share a fun way of how I motivated hostesses to participate in showing their catalog prior to their shows.

"Linda, about a third to a half of the guests you invite will actually attend. But whether we have three guests or twenty guests, we're going to have a great time, right?!"

"Of course!"

"My hostesses usually take several outside orders from guests who cannot attend their show. What this does is give you a lot of extra credit towards your show. You have one simple job—just ask! If you had been unable to attend Judy's show, would you have looked at the catalog if she asked you?"

"Sure!"

"As you invite and remind your guests about your show, it's inevitable that you'll hear objections from some of your guests concerning the date. It's part of living in the new millennium. When it's clear that your guests cannot attend the show, invite them to look at a catalog. Simply share that you are working on earning a Hostess Gift (describe it to her.) Then, at that point, set up a time to connect with them and show your catalog."

Complete the outside order conversation by giving your hostess an outside order form. Tell her about the customer specials and payment options, and show her how to write up an outside order.

7. Outside bookings (5 minutes).

The statistics are that if your hostess asks five of her friends to book a party before her show, she will procure at least one outside booking. The challenge is getting your hostess to ask.

For years I wondered, *"How do I encourage my hostesses to promote outside bookings?"* Why is it we so often miss the obvious?

Through trial and error, I finally identified the primary reason a hostess procures outside bookings prior to her show: ***someone tells her how to do it!***

Yes, hostesses who are educated on how to ask for a booking are the ones who most often do.

First, remind her what she earns for bookings. Second, give her an *example* of how to ask. Third, share a story of a hostess who had an outside booking or two. As I was concluding my message on outside bookings, I would often share this with my hostess.

"Karen, when you're checking in with your friends a couple days prior to your party, you will probably have a guest or two who will express disappointment about not being able to attend your party. Just invite them to have their own party and share your reasons for hosting a show. Tell them you're working on an outside booking and give them an idea of what they'll earn for hosting a show."

If your hostess is motivated and has her eye on a gift that requires bookings, it's your job to tell her how to earn it. Some hostesses are champing at the bit! Why? They're totally focused on a booking gift offered by the company. *In the Person-to-Person Hostess Coaching, don't sell your products; sell the booking gifts.* Booking gifts are sold to the hostess as a future possibility, a vision.

Sometimes *guests* want a booking gift, and when they find out they can't just buy it, they say, *"I'm not really sure I want to have a party. Besides I know I won't be able to get enough bookings from my friends."* My response was always to joke, *"Well, you've never had a party with me. No problem, the gift is yours! We'll do it together!"*

If a guest schedules a show because they want a booking gift, and you follow through with an effective Person-to-Person Coaching appointment and a fun show, chances are very good you'll secure three bookings. The bottom line is to keep it light, and invite your hostesses to "just ask!"

8. The "You Go, Girl!" Goal (5 minutes).

Sounds trendy, doesn't it? Make it natural and remember, it's all about the hostess. The You Go, Girl! Goal concluded my Person-to-Person Coaching appointments with a laugh and a fun plan directing my hostess to successful action.

"So, Janie, are you ready for the You Go, Girl! Goal?"

"The what, Steve?"

"The You Go, Girl! Goal, Janie."

"Steve, what's the You Go, Girl! Goal?"

"Janie, the You Go, Girl! Goal is a formula that I created that will ensure a successful show with a lot of free product for you.

Before I share the You Go, Girl! Goal, I want you to know that I am committed to your show whether two guests show up or twenty guests show up. I sincerely appreciate your support and I know (previous hostess) appreciates you, also.

I have a question for you. Which would be more exciting, $50 in free merchandise or $500 in free merchandise?"

"$500, of course, but I really just want to have a good time, and I don't want my friends to feel any pressure."

"Janie, I completely understand that, and let me reassure you that your friends will enjoy a good time with no pressure. It's just not how I work. In fact, I book lots of hostesses precisely because everyone has a good time.

The You Go, Girl! Goal is really just three very simple steps you can take to ensure a successful and fun show, both for us and for your guests. Here they are:

1. Call all guests one or two days prior to your party. Everyone loves to feel special. Make it fun! As you call your guests, tell them they made your Top Ten List, and that it would mean the world to you to have them at your party.

Focus on having ten guests in attendance. Invite each guest to bring a friend. Ask,

"Mary, don't you have a friend you'd like to spend the evening with, maybe someone you haven't thought of in a while?" Then tell her to invite her friend to your party because it will give them a chance to catch up and you're guaranteeing a fun (theme name) and a good time.

2. Focus on five outside orders. As some of your guests express their regret about having to pass up your fun Friends' Night Out experience, invite them to take a look at the catalog prior to your show. Schedule a time to take their order. This will make your party a success before it even begins!

3. Secure one outside booking. As I shared with you earlier, you will inevitably receive a call or two from guests who are already collectors of my product. Those are the ones to invite to host their own party. Offer them (*credit or other incentive*) and remember to tell them what you earn if they schedule a show."

The You Go, Girl! Goal can be called anything you choose. What resonates with you? What is your signature phrase? For fifteen years, my wife has been using a phrase that is completely unique to her. She calls it the "Sticky Dow Wow" goal. The point is to make it fun and *you*!

We're almost complete! What has transpired thus far in our hostess coaching experience?

> You have arrived at the Person-to-Person Coaching appointment five minutes early.
>
> You've enjoyed ten to fifteen minutes getting to know the hostess and gathering information through relationally focused and universal listening.
>
> You have collected a guest invitation list and postage and have prepared the hostess to achieve and enjoy a successful show.
>
> You've planted recruiting seeds throughout the coaching appointment and now you're ready to "share the business."

The Powerful Conclusion to the Person-to-Person Coaching Appointment

Years ago, Lynn and I held a brainstorming session with a few of our executive managers on the subject of recruiting and development. We discussed a questionnaire, sent out by our executive staff, which essentially consisted of one basic question: *Where did the interest originate with each individual recruit whom you have introduced to our company within the last 6 months? Did it originate at a show, cold call, hostess coaching, referral, personal showing, or "other"?*

We asked the managers to list all their recruits and circle the answer that matched each individual recruit. To our surprise, 87% of the representatives in our organization reported that the initial interest of their recruits originated at the hostess coaching experience.

This survey increased our curiosity and engendered further research. Our executive managers polled the entire organization, asking, *"What percentage of hostesses do you hostess coach?"*

An analysis of the responses concluded that a whopping 42% of all hostesses being booked in our organization were being coached in person. The results seemed to indicate that many of our part-time representatives and what I call "play-time" representatives coached *occasionally.* (Personally, I questioned that. I have found that either you tend to coach or you don't.)

The results also revealed that the most successful recruiters were coaching *97% of the time.* That statistic gave us insight as to our management's future direction. It became our focus to train our representatives in all aspects of hostess coaching, and in that year, my income increased 30% from the previous year.

Isn't it amazing how life works? When we get curious and ask questions, the answers light up like a neon sign. The huge message behind this statistic was the importance of focusing on sharing the business opportunity *at the hostess coaching.*

Previously, although I discussed the business with some of my hostesses, I can't say it was consistently a part of each and every hostess coaching appointment. After the survey, a larger vision, the conclusion of the Person-to-Person Coaching experience, was born.

9. Share the business (10-20 minutes).

The basic agenda during this period is:

- to share the benefits of the business as you have experienced them and as they are outlined in your recruiting material
- to tell your own personal story
- to ask for referrals, and
- to invite your hostess to a local event.

What *is* your story? Have you ever written it down on paper? Have you ever crafted it in a way that is brief, truthful, and authentic, *and* contains recruiting seeds and power statements?

And then, have you practiced speaking it in front of your family or your best friend until it becomes comfortable? It is through the activity of practicing that we reach our full capacity.

The last and most powerful part of the Person-to-Person Coaching experience is sharing your story, asking for a referral, and inviting your hostess to take a look at the business. As you read my story, I invite you to envision your own authentic story and the endless possibilities that could become reality by committing to our in-depth training.

"Jan, by now, you must realize that I sincerely enjoy my career. Part of the reason I'm in this business is to make a difference in our community by offering this great opportunity. So many times I have seen (*company name*) have an impact on lives beyond financial earnings with benefits like all-expense-paid vacations, diamonds, awards, and more personal rewards such as development of communication skills and self-esteem. I want to give you an opportunity to earn a special item from my 'special stock' for referring someone you feel would be talented in my line of work. We all have friends who have *more month left over at the end of the money* or who have given up their careers to stay home with their children and might be looking for an outlet like (*company name*). It gives me great pleasure to be able to offer someone an opportunity to make $30 an hour part-time or even $50--$100 thousand a year."

I personally started in this industry at the age of 17 because I didn't have the money to go to school, and in 1983 I made $24,500 part-time while attending college full-time. After my second year of college (and four all-expense-paid vacations, I might add) I realized that this was the work that gave me true fulfillment. I love entertaining others and feeling like the sky's the limit! For most people this industry is a lucrative part-time business, a great tax write off or a fun hobby where they can make money instead of spending it. Who do you know who has talent with people and loves to entertain and you feel might enjoy taking a look at what we offer?"

At this point, most of my hostesses were asking me questions or naming friends who fit the description. Occasionally my hostess would reply with a big, *"Me! I fit the description!"*

Whether I received a reaction or not, I always ended with this question, *"Have you ever thought about doing what I do?"* As you ask this question with confidence and genuine curiosity, time and time again you will find yourself surprised at the responses you receive from your hostesses.

Thankfully, I stick to business principles rather than acting solely on my own perception, experience, or judgment! I have recruited hostesses I would have bet money had no interest, much less would have actually joined. In fact, one of my sleeper recruits is the editor of this book. Lynda started the business and went on to earn the award as the #1 sales representative in personal sales at the company convention.

And Lynda has played an even deeper role in my life, reminding me of the benefits of being open and present with hostesses and guests. Life is bigger than we imagine. We can pass up unbelievable possibilities if we allow our own fears or judgments to rule our actions.

EXERCISE 2

Take time now to create your own story, as you will relate it during your Person-to-Person Coaching. Understand that you will probably continue to refine this version of your story as you grow in your business. The longest journey begins with the first step; so for now, follow these steps.

1. First, decide what you honestly want to communicate to your hostess and then write it down.

2. Read your story out loud several times and reword it as you become aware of better or more natural ways to express yourself.

3. Now, close your eyes. Imagine yourself in a large suburban living room with your new hostess.

What is it like?

Where are you sitting?

What kind of furniture is there?

With your eyes still closed, practice telling your story. Follow the same procedure imagining unfamiliar surroundings: a restaurant, a one-bedroom apartment, etc.

4. Practice your story with a family member or friend. If you wish, ask for their feedback. Continue practicing until you feel comfortable that your presentation is thoroughly natural, truthful, and phrased just the way you want it.

The conclusion of your Person-to-Person Coaching appointment is simply to invite your hostess to the next local event as an opportunity to have fun and take a look at your company or to introduce a friend she feels may have interest.

For best results, create an invitation, or ask your leader for a flyer on the upcoming events being offered by your local organization.

In our business we have the opportunity to give of ourselves. As I've said before, giving is part of our basic nature. As we give, we feel more alive and participate more fully in our individual lives and businesses.

All the elements of the Person-to-Person Coaching experience are designed to provide an opportunity for you to partner with your hostesses in achieving mutually beneficial results.

Being open and real creates the possibility for such a relationship to develop and grow into untold success.

Share a part of yourself. Let go of focusing on how you look, whether or not you're saying the right thing, and whether your hostess will be interested or not. It's really not about you; it's about them. You simply become the beneficiary of the relationship when the answer is a huge "YES!"

"There is a vitality, a life force, a quickening
that is translated through you into action,
and
because there is only one of you in all time,
this expression is unique.
If you block it, it will never exist.
It will be lost to the world."

—Anonymous

Person-to-Person Coaching: A Choice

In just a few pages you will have learned every dimension of the Person-to-Person Coaching experience and will arrive at a place where you choose to commit to the program or not.

Each of us can find excuses not to coach because of location, personal agendas, or time. There may be many objections that hold you back from making this commitment. I invite you to consider that the *quality* of Person-to-Person Coaching may give you greater success than *quantity* can give you in your present situation.

If you're up against serious circumstances, at least coach those guests who have expressed interest or you feel would be talented in your business. Find a way to work within the circumstance. Perhaps they could join you in your own home for a cup of coffee. **The important thing is to make the connection.**

While we are able to control our choice of actions, we cannot control the consequences of our choices—universal laws and principles do.

If your choice of action was to hold only parties that were coached and had a returned list, what do you believe would be the outcome? Would universal laws and principles govern success?

I'm convinced that the masters in personal sales, recruiting, and in life outside their careers would agree that this method *will* create success in all aspects of the business.

Let's face it, if a hostess is willing to meet with you in person to plan her show, don't you agree that the show will be more successful than if it were coached weeks ago at the original show, on the phone, or not at all? And isn't it true that you're more likely to recruit her if you have coached her and shared the business with her in person prior to her show?

I know beyond a shadow of a doubt your hostesses who meet you within a week to plan their parties and submit their lists will excel beyond your expectations.

Wouldn't you rather do one less show a week and have a smooth schedule with excellent returns and fulfilling relationships with your hostesses than chaos, ups and downs, and uncertainty? Unless the hostess is an hour away, it's Person-to-Person Coaching or no party!

Obviously, life isn't black and white. Sometimes you may need to accept Plan B, coaching over the phone and accepting a faxed list, but instances will be rare as long as you commit to valuing and upholding this practice.

Successful business practices are based on universal laws and principles that govern success. The benefit to us is confidence, calmness, and greater ease in day-to-day decision-making.

I have observed many successful representatives in this industry. Those who have incorporated these practices have encountered growth and stability, while authentically enjoying themselves. Those who have simply drifted along the way may have garnered short-term success, but not without chaos and instability.

A few years ago, I watched two leaders who both had extraordinary talent in selling, booking and recruiting. Yet, they had totally different experiences. Each leader had a very high show average; each was extremely successful in booking and recruiting. The noticeable difference was one leader coached all her hostesses utilizing these business principles, and the other did not.

The one who coached was extremely *consistent*, selling approximately the same every week. She *consistently* recruited, and her group's volume *consistently* increased. She never appeared overwhelmed or frantic. In fact, she lives a very balanced life.

The other leader, who chose not to coach, experienced cancellations and rescheduled shows on a regular basis. Some weeks she was #1 in sales and other weeks she did zero in sales. This leader's recruit leads often said yes to the business but seemed to "slip out" of training.

Most importantly, as a person, this leader always sounded disappointed, exhausted, and overwhelmed. She claimed it was the hostesses' fault. Which leader do you want to emulate? It's your choice.

More important than how fast you're going is where you're headed.

If there is one message I want you to absorb, it is that a meaningful life is not a matter of speed. It's about what you do and why you do it.

Do you want meaningful relationships in your business? Do you want extraordinary results? Do you want a future with your company? If you answered yes to each of these questions, my mission is complete.

Coach Person-to-Person!

Appendices

Appendix 1

What Is Coaching And Why Does It Work?

Coaching is a unique relationship forged by coach and client for the sole purpose of accelerating the client's progress in her or his personal and professional life. Coach and client together design a powerful alliance that is completely customized to the individual. Unlike counseling or therapy, which focus on delving into and discovering the meaning of the past, coaching focuses on where you are today and how to get where you want to be tomorrow.

Coaching works. Coaches believe their clients are already naturally creative, resourceful, and whole. What does that mean? It means you have the answers within you, and with the help of your coach, you will discover them.

- You will be able to define exactly what you want, even if you think you have no idea when you begin.

- You will create strategies for dealing with roadblocks and limitations.

- You will devise a plan of action that is practical, doable, and is based on your own truth.

- You will move into action, fully supported and cheered on by your coach, who will hold you accountable for your commitments even when you feel you may have lost sight of your goal.

How do these amazing results occur? It's in the coaching relationship, which is unlike any other you have ever had. Your coach is 100% there for you, completely committed to your success. You may have friends who love and support you, but with your coach, ***every*** interaction is all about and for ***you***.

Coaching provides a safe place to explore the unthinkable and reach for the impossible—a place to discover or re-discover your own truest values and develop a life that honors who you are. Your coach will call forth your greatness and help you live it in the world.

Appendix 2

Coaching Direct Sales Professionals

According to the Direct Sales Association, estimated U.S. direct sales for 2000 totaled over 25 billion dollars. The industry is limitless! Individuals can literally write their own paychecks, set their own hours, and within company parameters, make their own rules. Then why are more representatives failing than succeeding?

Of course, there are many variables at work within and outside the industry. But one thing is certain: leaders are constantly looking for ways to help their organization, and representatives are searching for ways to build their businesses. Both are looking for greater returns.

- What's stopping you from taking your business to the next level?
- If you could achieve your ultimate vision for your life and business within one year, what would you experience?
- What would it be worth to you to break through the barriers that are

keeping you from creating your ideal life and business?

Our coaches have over 35 years combined experience in the direct sales field. They know that personal and business coaching is the ideal way to identify the blocks that are separating you from success, while at the same time creating the vision and plan that supports your WHOLE life.

Although your company and leaders can teach you how to book, sell, and recruit, they cannot teach you how to live your life. You already have your own interior blueprint that is ideal for you. Coaching evokes your greatest vision and truest values, and it provides the training and tools to design the road map that will take you to your ultimate destination.

The coaches at **Lifeline Coaching and Education, Inc.** will customize a program that is specifically suited to your needs, based on your current level of knowledge and expertise. **Lifeline Coaching and Education, Inc.** has a sincere desire to bring you abundance. Watch your business grow beyond your wildest expectations when you follow the principles in our Direct Sales program.

Appendix 3

About Lifeline Coaching and Education, Inc.

We believe that representatives in the direct sales industry comprise one community.

Our mission is to educate and empower those representatives to realize their deepest intention.

Our purpose is to partner with each individual, holding them accountable as they develop a clearly defined course of action.

We do this by guiding them toward consistent results, leading them to clarity and commitment, and supporting them in achieving balance and fulfillment.

Lifeline Coaching and Education, Inc. is incorporated in the State of Oregon.

Order Information

Also by Steve Wiltshire:

Vision Made Real:
Creating Space for Your Deepest Intention

Systems 101:
The Inner Workings of Direct Sales

To order more copies of *Partnering With Your Hostess* or other publications by Steve Wiltshire contact Lifeline Press at the address below:

Partnering
c/o Lifeline Press
2738 NE 9th Avenue
Portland, OR 97212

Or email us at:

support@lifelinecoaches.com

Visit our Website!

You may also order online at:

www.LifelineCoaches.com